WINDOWS OF WORSHIP™

purpose

purpose

WINDOWS OF WORSHIP™

When I'm
SEEKING GOD'S WILL

:: DEVOTIONAL JOURNAL ::

Greg Allen ▪ Rick Rusaw ▪ Dan Stuecher
Paul S. Williams, *Editor*

Standard
PUBLISHING

© 2004 CNI Holdings Corp., Windows of Worship is a Trademark of
Christian Network, Inc.

Published by Standard Publishing, Cincinnati, Ohio. A division of Standex
International Corporation. Printed in China.

Cover and interior design by Rule29.

Discover where to watch *Worship* in your town by logging on to
www.Worship.net.

ISBN 0-7847-1514-9

09 08 07 06 05 04   9 8 7 6 5 4 3 2 1

We were made to worship...

The first song I remember Grandma Stone singing to me was "Jesus Loves Me." As a three-year-old I sat on her lap on the front porch swing and asked her to sing it over and over again. Before my daughter Jana could speak, she hummed the same tune, its melody unmistakable as she played on the family room floor. We were made to worship.

To worship God is to walk through the shadows into a familiar welcoming place, where the fire never dies and the light is soft and glowing. To worship God is to know we are truly home, acting on a desire deep in our souls. Long before we rationally understand the truth of Christ, we want to praise someone or something for bringing love and beauty, joy and hope into the world.

At the Christian Network, our desire is simple. Whether through the written page or the television screen, we hope these words and images will draw you to worship, as we thank our Creator for breathing life and love into his creation.

PAUL S. WILLIAMS
Chairman of the Board of Stewards
The Christian Network, Inc.

Be of Value

Never be lacking in zeal, but keep your spiritual fervor, serving the Lord. Be joyful in hope, patient in affliction, faithful in prayer.

ROMANS 12:11, 12

BE OF VALUE

I had just moved from my home in upstate New York to Ft. Myers, Florida, to begin my first job in a local church. It was a wonderful place with real opportunities. But I also had plenty of dreams for the future that stretched far beyond the confines of that first Florida church. I was very ambitious. And while ambition can be healthy, ambition clothed in immaturity can be disastrous.

There was an 80-year-old minister on staff at that Florida church. His name was Dr. Lester Ford. Dr. Ford had been an engineer, preacher, and college president. He had moved to Florida to retire, but a few days a week he gave his time to the church. And I have no idea why, but Dr. Ford took me under his wing.

One day at lunch he asked me what I wanted to do with my life. With plenty of enthusiasm I shared the dreams on my heart. Dr. Ford listened carefully. He helped me shape my ideas. He encouraged many, and he smiled or laughed at some, as though they were distantly familiar to him. After a long time, Dr. Ford leaned across the table and said to me, "Rick, you have plenty of great dreams, and you should never stop dreaming, but along the way, learn to be of value where you are. Because if you don't learn to do that, you won't have much of a future. And you can't be of value somewhere you're not."

"Be of value where you are." That was the advice the retired minister gave me. It was OK to dream about tomorrow, as long as I was giving energy, passion, and prayer to what I was doing today.

As the years have gone by, a lot of the dreams I shared with Dr. Ford have come true. I have viewed the fulfillment of those dreams as precious gifts—gifts that arrived when I chose to be faithful through difficult times, to be of value where I was.

Dr. Ford went to be with the Father a long time ago. On one of our last visits I thanked him for his friendship and his investment in me. He smiled, took my hand, and looked me straight in the eye. "Just be of value where you are, Rick," he said, "because you never know what God has in store."

—*Rick Rusaw*

What are your hopes, dreams, and ambitions for your future?
Write out some of them.

_____

_____

_____

_____

_____

8

_____

_____

_____

_____

_____

_____

_____

_____

As you look to the future, remember to look around you for opportunities now. What are some specific ways you can "be of value where you are"?

_____

_____

_____

_____

_____

_____

_____

_____

_____

_____

_____

_____

_____

On Using Power, or Not

Your attitude should be the same as that of Christ Jesus:

Who, being in very nature God,

did not consider equality with God something to be grasped,

but made himself nothing,

taking the very nature of a servant,

being made in human likeness.

And being found in appearance as a man,

he humbled himself

and became obedient to death—

even death on a cross!

PHILIPPIANS 2:5–8

ON USING POWER, OR NOT

I ran about an hour in the park yesterday. I've been running for 25 years now. I figure that sometime last year I passed 20,000 miles. When my son Jonathan was young, he liked to go running with me. He'd say, "Can I go running with ya, Dad?" I'd say, "Sure." He'd take off running as fast as his 4-year-old legs could take him, and I'd run slower than I can walk. That's hard to do. After about a quarter of a mile he'd say "I'm kinda tuckered out now, Dad. Do you mind if we head back home?"

Now I had the power to totally obliterate my son, to leave him coughing and sputtering in the dust—a speck in the distance. But I love my son. And my love caused me to restrain the power I had in order to run at his speed, so he could feel good about himself. So he could say, "I'm a runner. I run with my daddy." It was not my power that was important. It was my willingness not to use the power I had.

The disciples of Jesus were eager for him to become the new political king of Israel, defeat the blasted Romans, and give them free food, a loaf of Roman Meal bread every morning. But Jesus had a different idea. He said to his disciples, "Whoever wants to become great among you must be your servant, and whoever wants to be first must be your slave" (Matthew 20:26, 27). That blew them right out of their sandals. Virtually everyone in their culture grabbed all the power they could get and didn't let go, no matter what. Then Jesus came along and said just the opposite. It's not about grabbing power. It's about channeling the power you have into acts of service.

Jonathan is 26 years old now. We went hiking in Rocky Mountain National Park last year. We decided to run up a trail to Gem Lake. It's about 1.6 miles long, with an elevation gain of about 1,000 feet. The trail ends at an altitude of 9,000 feet.

We started running and Jonathan took off. He left me coughing and sputtering in the dust—a speck in the distance. Then about the time we got to the top of the first rise, I noticed I was catching up. Before long I pulled up beside him and said, "Went out too fast, huh?" He said, "Yeah, I guess so." But then I noticed he wasn't breathing hard; he was barely sweating. He was practicing a principle he had learned long ago. He was restraining the power he had, running at his dad's speed, so his dad could feel good about himself. So I could say, "I ran up the mountain with my son." It wasn't his power that was important. It was his willingness not to use the power he had.

13

—Paul S. Williams

Have you ever purposely limited your "power" for the sake of someone else (let a child win a game, forgave someone graciously when you had every right to vent your anger instead)? What was your purpose in doing so?

_____

_____

_____

_____

_____

_____

_____

_____

_____

_____

_____

_____

Think about Jesus. List some of the powers he gave up when he came to Earth. Why do you think he did it? How does it make you feel to realize what he did for you?

_____

_____

_____

_____

_____

_____

_____

_____

_____

_____

_____

_____

_____

This Is Holy Ground

We ask you, brothers, to respect those who work hard among you,

who are over you in the Lord and who admonish you. Hold them

in the highest regard in love because of their work.

1 THeSSALONIANS 5:12, 13

THIS IS HOLY GROUND

"Shed your shoes," God said to Moses. "You're standing on holy ground."

Probably the most amazing thing to Moses wasn't hearing the voice of God or seeing a burning bush that would not be consumed. According to David Whyte in his book, *Crossing the Unknown Sea*, the most amazing thing to Moses was looking down and seeing that it was ordinary dirt he was standing on. The "holy ground" had been beneath his feet for 80 years. Only now, he saw that it was indeed holy—every cubic inch of it.

All of us who are preachers, long-term practitioners of the faith in cities and towns spread across the United States, hold one thing in common. We know we are standing on holy ground.

It's not the church building that makes the ground holy. It's not because we stand behind a pulpit that we have that distinction. You are standing on holy ground too. It is the condition of all who are made in the image of the creator. The preacher's job has always been the same, whether 800 years ago or last Sunday. The preacher's job is to help us look down at our feet and realize the dust covering our wingtips is tinged with eternity's gold.

This life we inhabit is neither a plaything nor a random breathing machine. It is a soul, enmeshed with sinew, skin, and bone, and from the time of its birth, it is longing for its true home. The journey toward that home is holy—every dusty mile of it.

For centuries, people have publicly preached the truth of Christ. If you looked carefully, you would have seen that behind their robes, they were all trembling—every last one of them. The same is true in every church on every Sunday in every nation. Behind the suit, behind the vestments, behind the polo shirt, knees are knocking. Why? Because the preacher knows he is speaking holy words.

But one other thing they know as well. They know that, if their hearts are turned steadfastly toward the gospel, their ears tuned to the still, small voice, and their eyes firmly focused on the holy ground beneath their feet, their voices will speak truth with beauty and grace and laughter.

—Paul S. Williams

19

Think of the ministers you have known in your life. What specific things did you learn from each one?

_____

_____

_____

_____

_____

_____

_____

_____

_____

_____

_____

_____

List some specific ways you can encourage the ministers who
are in your life now. How can you show them your appreciation
for guiding you in your walk with Jesus?

_____

_____

_____

_____

_____

_____

_____

_____

_____

_____

_____

_____

_____

God's Open Door

You are all sons of God through faith in Christ Jesus, for all of you

who were baptized into Christ have clothed yourselves with Christ.

There is neither Jew nor Greek, slave nor free, male nor female,

for you are all one in Christ Jesus.

GALATIANS 3:26–28

GOD'S OPEN DOOR

Harold and Jane thought that winning a Caribbean cruise was the best thing that ever happened to them. All they did was put their names in a big glass bowl at the local county fair. It was the first time either of them had ever won anything.

Their friends couldn't wait to hear what the lucky couple had to say when they got home. But as things turned out, the trip was not all they thought it would be. Oh, the food was good. The entertainment was professional. But, though they tried to talk with people and make friends, they just never connected with anyone. Coming from a small country town, they felt out of place. As Harold put it, "We had nothing in common with our fellow-passengers. They were all there because they were wealthy. We were there because we were lucky."

Have you ever felt out of place? You're not alone. A lot of people feel that way. Our world tends to be divided between the "haves" and the "have-nots"—the movers and the shakers and those who are moved and shaken.

When he chose to reach out to fallen humanity, God chose to start with the bottom rungs of the social ladder, not the top ones. When God's chosen people were looking for a rich and powerful king to be their Savior—their Messiah—they got a helpless baby instead, born not into a five-bedroom home with a three-car garage, but in a barn. No custom-made crib, just an animal trough. No luxury car, just a donkey.

Jesus surprised many by spending time with the outcasts of society—the destitute, the unwanted, those who were hard to love. And Jesus said to his followers, "Whatever you did for . . . the least of these, you did for me" (Matthew 25:40).

That doesn't mean people should feel guilty for the things they own or the status they've achieved. The clear message of Scripture is that God's kingdom is open to everyone. No one should ever feel he doesn't belong. Oh, there are churches that come across as if they are closed to certain kinds of people. Maybe you've been to a few. But God's doors are open wide. If the kingdom of God is a party, then everyone is invited, all are welcome. It does not matter what kind of car you drive or what kind of clothes you wear. God's kingdom—God's great, joyful party—is for you, no matter what others might think of you or what you think of yourself. You are welcome. God's door is always open.

—*Greg Allen*

Where are the places you don't feel you belong? What causes you to feel that way?

_____

_____

_____

_____

_____

_____

_____

_____

_____

_____

_____

_____

_____

Do you know people who feel out of place? What can you do to pass on God's acceptance and love to those people to help them feel that they belong?

The Sound of Confession

You, O God, do see trouble and grief;

> *you consider it to take it in hand.*

The victim commits himself to you;

> *you are the helper of the fatherless. . . .*

You hear, O LORD, the desire of the afflicted;

> *you encourage them, and you listen to their cry,*

defending the fatherless and the oppressed,

> *in order that man, who is of the earth, may terrify no more.*

PSALM 10:14, 17, 18

THE SOUND OF CONFESSION

In Vienna there is always music. Every Sunday, the finest music ever composed is available free of charge in cathedrals throughout the city. Shortly after World War I, a college student named Maria Kutschera made her rounds from church to church, taking advantage of all these free performances. One day in the heart of Vienna, Maria saw a huge crowd gathering at a Jesuit church. "Ah," she thought, "Palm Sunday. It can only mean Bach." But there was no music that morning—just a sermon. She found herself trapped by the crowd, unable to escape from the church.

The message, delivered by a popular Jesuit preacher, made her angry. She had been raised in the church, but she had given up her belief in God years before. After the service, she found the priest, grabbed him by the arm and said loudly, "How can you believe all this?" What the priest said in response changed her life forever.

Maria had an unhappy childhood. Her mother had died of pneumonia when she was very small, and she was placed in the care of an elderly cousin. Her father, who saw her only occasionally, died before she became a teenager. An abusive uncle took over raising her, and she lost all faith in the redeeming nature of life. Eventually she ran away and worked various jobs until she saved enough money for college. And now she was outside a church, angrily confronting a Jesuit priest about his belief in a loving God. His simple response to Maria's angry confrontation was: "Meet me here Tuesday at 4:00."

Tuesday came, and for more than two hours Maria gave the priest every accusation against God she had ever learned. When she finished the priest didn't say a word; he just looked at her with disciplined silence. She thought of more things to say. Again, he responded by saying nothing. Eventually Maria ran out of accusations, and it was then, and only then, that the priest finally spoke. "Well, my dear," he said, "you simply have been wrongly informed." Realizing she had once been a practicing Catholic he asked her, "When did you last go to confession?" She was completely disarmed by his unwillingness to acknowledge her doubt. Instead, the Jesuit received her mad ranting as a confession. "Take courage," he said. "I am going to pronounce the words, 'thy sins are forgiven . . .' God will forget them, and your soul will look like the soul of a newly baptized person."

When he said the words, Maria found all of her arguments and hostility melting away. She felt as if she was "floating on a cloud." Confession was indeed good for the soul. Maria became so zealous that she decided to join a convent, though her time there didn't last long. Her story from this point might seem very familiar, for Maria Kutschera eventually became Maria Von Trapp—the young lady whose life is forever immortalized in the classic film, *The Sound of Music*.

And it was all because of a patient priest, who knew when to speak and when not to speak, gently guiding a lost child until she found her way home.

—*Eric Snyder for Paul S. Williams*

What circumstances in your life have caused you to be angry with God? Confess them in writing here.

_____

_____

_____

_____

_____

_____

_____

_____

_____

_____

_____

_____

Write a prayer, pouring out all your feelings to God. Ask him to bring you his presence and peace in the midst of your anger.

_____

_____

_____

_____

_____

_____

33

_____

_____

_____

_____

_____

_____

_____

_____

Stretcher

*Carry each other's burdens, and in this way you will fulfill the
law of Christ.*

GALATIANS 6:2

STRETCHER

We could all use a friend like this, because he was nothing if not persistent.

Jesus was teaching in a house in the town of Capernaum. Crowds of people had gathered to hear him. You can picture the scene—people jammed in the living room, leaning in the windows, spilling out into the street. Rumor had already spread that Jesus not only had amazing things to say, but that he also was doing some amazing deeds. People who were blind, deaf, and suffering form other disabilities, were healed.

Now there was a man with a disability who had some very good friends. They knew if they could get their friend to Jesus, then just maybe he would walk again. No guarantees, no promises; but they believed that Jesus would do what they wanted him to do—try.

When they realized they couldn't even get close to the house, let alone see Jesus, they must have been disappointed. But at least one of these stretcher bearers wasn't about to be deterred. Before you knew it, he and the disabled man were on top of the house; the friends were breaking through the hard clay of the rooftop and lowering their friend on his stretcher through the roof.

At this point, if you are the man on the stretcher, you must be asking yourself if this is really a good idea. You wonder if Jesus will toss you out or criticize your friends for their recklessness. But before the man could utter an apology, Jesus commended the faithfulness of his friends and invited him to walk. You can only imagine how grateful the guy must have been for friends like that.

I can't help but read this story and be grateful for those who've carried the stretcher for me. It's likely someone has carried the stretcher for you too. It could have been a family member who prayed for you or a parent who took you to church. It may have been a friend whose example drew you closer to God. If life has been at all good to you, you can be sure someone carried the stretcher for you. Drop that person a note or find another way to say thanks. Then find a stretcher you can carry. You never know what will happen when you help someone meet Jesus.

—Rick Rusaw

List the people who have "carried the stretcher" for you. How
did each of them minister to you?

_____

_____

_____

_____

_____

_____

_____

_____

_____

_____

_____

_____

_____

_____

List people you have carried. What things did you do? Who else in your life might need a stretcher bearer today?

_____

_____

_____

_____

_____

_____

_____

_____

_____

_____

_____

_____

_____

_____

purpose

Rejoice and Be Glad

Blessed are those who are persecuted because of righteousness,

for theirs is the kingdom of heaven. Blessed are you when people

insult you, persecute you and falsely say all kinds of evil against

you because of me. Rejoice and be glad, because great is your

reward in heaven, for in the same way they persecuted the

prophets who were before you.

MATTHEW 5:10–12

REJOICE AND BE GLAD

There were many influential people who recognized the remarkable talent of Gustav Mahler, the world's greatest symphony conductor at the turn of the 20th century. They personally supported him, recommended him for prestigious positions of leadership in the key music centers of Europe, and generally facilitated his rise to prominence. That's usually the case for each of us in our own spiritual journey, isn't it? We're all indebted to those individuals who love us and believe in us, on whose shoulders we stand.

But there is nearly always a flip side to that truth. Most of us have our detractors who, for one reason or another, seem committed to doing their very best to complicate our lives by any means possible. Mahler certainly had detractors. One incident in particular sheds some interesting light on why most of us have to deal with these negative characters.

Born into a Jewish family in the midst of poverty, Gustav Mahler would develop into a remarkable talent and a very interesting man. He inspired support and encouragement from numerous influential people. He was just 23 years old when one such friend secured a position for him as second conductor at the Royal Prussian Court Theater in Kassel, Germany. But it would be a rocky experience. Keep in mind that the position was "second conductor." The first conductor, Wilhelm Treiber, was an older man given to an autocratic style of leadership and, as is often the case, he was easily threatened because of his own insecurities.

Shortly after Mahler was hired, city officials announced plans for a four-day music festival in Kassel, and they appointed Mahler as director. It would be a wonderful opportunity! Treiber would be responsible for several rehearsals, and that's when the trouble began. Furious from not having been assigned the director's task, and already quite envious of the young new conductor, the jealous older man began to sow discord among the musicians, turning them against Mahler. The orchestra refused to play under Mahler's baton. Now he was faced with the daunting task of locating players to replace those who had quit.

Not one to admit defeat, he scoured all of Germany and in an unbelievably short time came up with the necessary musicians, going so far as to recruit a small military band from a local infantry unit. Mahler would work the players hard, spurring them on to the challenge of being prepared on such short notice. It paid off. The event was a huge success and would catapult Mahler to realize his greatest dream, to become the principal conductor and director of the Imperial Opera in Vienna. Treiber, on the other hand, would fade into obscurity.

Gustav Mahler avoided being distracted by malicious attempts to undermine him by simply focusing his efforts on the task at hand. I am deeply indebted to young Mahler for such a powerful example.

43

Jesus made it very clear to all of us that we will pay a price for identifying our lives in him. We will have our detractors. There will be those people who won't like us because of him. When we pursue his purposes for us, these self-proclaimed rivals will do everything possible to hinder us. They may even get nasty. That's exactly when Jesus tells us to laugh it off. "Rejoice and be glad," he said. Stay the course. Remain focused. Continue devoting yourself to the task he's given you, and after he has enabled you to succeed and move on to greater things, those angry, envious, ill-mannered adversaries will be nowhere in sight.

—Dan Stuecher

Name the people who have helped you along your life's journey by believing in you and encouraging you. List people whom you could help in the same way.

_____

_____

_____

_____

_____

_____

_____

_____

_____

_____

_____

_____

_____

Name the people who have been your detractors. Pray for each
of them. Have *you* been a discouraging figure in anyone's life?
Ask God to show you how you might change from a discourager
to an encourager.

Cloud-Watching

Be strong and do not give up, for your work will be rewarded.

2 Chronicles 15:7

CLOUD-WATCHING

The citizens of the state of New York approached President Thomas Jefferson about an idea of building a canal that would reach across the entire state. Jefferson said, "That is a marvelous idea and something that should be done . . . a hundred years from now." The cost for such a canal would be around $7 million—equal to 3.5 billion dollars today. The most vocal leader of the canal movement was the mayor of New York City, De Witt Clinton. He and many others believed that a canal connecting the western frontier with the city in the east would bring prosperity to the entire state. The federal government thought he was crazy, and for once the press agreed.

By 1811 there were ominous clouds on the horizon that made the canal totally impractical. The following year our small country would once again be at war with the British Empire. And with such problems facing our fledgling government, the idea of building a canal was ruled out of the question; that is, until the people of New York state decided to build it themselves.

Now it is important to note that, at the time, there were no engineering schools in the country to offer any expertise. All 363 miles of the canal would be dug by hand, 40 feet wide and four feet deep. And as predicted, five years into the project the canal was far from completed. The New York press lambasted the governor, calling the canal "Clinton's Ditch." The storm of criticism and protest resulted in De Witt Clinton being voted out of office and removed from the canal board. The whole project was beginning to look like a gigantic disaster.

Solomon wrote in Ecclesiastes 11:4, 6 that, "Whoever watches the wind will not plant; whoever looks at the clouds will not reap. . . . Sow your seed in the morning, and at evening let not your hands be idle, for you do not know which will succeed, whether this or that, or whether both will do equally well."

When the Erie Canal was nearly finished in 1825, it once again became in vogue with the citizens of New York. De Witt Clinton was voted back in office and regarded as a great visionary. Upon completion, the effect of the canal was immediate and dramatic, resulting in an explosion of trade and an age of prosperity. But it could just as easily have gone the other way. A natural disaster could have occurred. Another war could have broken out. The clouds of protest and warning might have been prophetic. Instead of looking like a genius, De Witt Clinton might have looked like a fool. We can imagine Solomon's word to fools and geniuses: "There will always be wind, and there will always be clouds. Build it anyway."

—Eric Snyder for Rick Rusaw

What is your "Erie Canal"—the thing that you are passionate about, in spite of what anyone thinks?

_____

_____

_____

_____

_____

_____

_____

_____

_____

_____

_____

_____

_____

_____

Commit this passion to God. Write out a prayer, telling God all about your dream. Then ask him to help you make it come true, if that is his will.

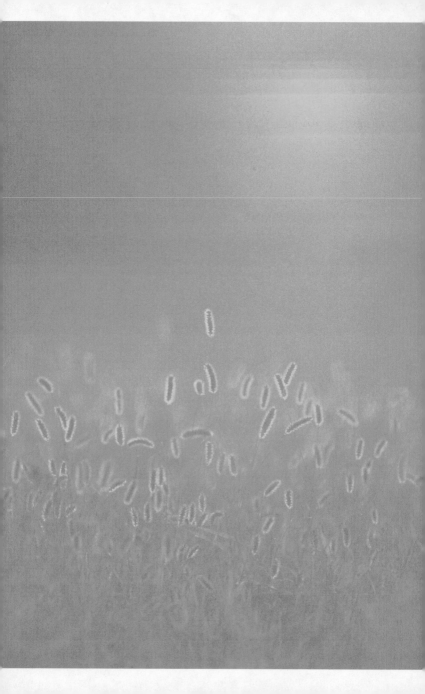

The Remains of the Fire

When you walk through the fire,

   you will not be burned;

   the flames will not set you ablaze.

For I am the LORD, your God,

   the Holy One of Israel, your Savior.

ISAIAH 43:2, 3

THE REMAINS OF THE FIRE

The songwriter Mark Heard claims that a holy war is loved by everybody. His words seem especially relevant in this day of boycotts, protests, and jihads. A crowd can become a righteous mob with a few stirring words about the evil people on the other side. What's interesting, though, is when you look at history the mob is rarely ever righteous. For the most part, the crowd pretty much goes with the flow. And every now and then a few brave individuals decide not to follow everybody else. We call them heroes now. They were heretics then. We don't give heretics fanfare. We give them fire.

The story of three young Hebrew men is told in the Bible, in the book of Daniel. The king of Babylon required all of his citizens to publicly pay homage to the image that he had created. To refuse to go with the king's program would be a crime punishable by death. Death by fire, to be exact. Now these young men were by no means troublemakers. They had already been kidnapped from their homeland and forced to become Babylonian subjects. They were even required to drop their family names and were given strange-sounding names instead: Shadrach, Meshach, and Abednego.

What the king was asking them to do now would not be physically painful. It would not be as difficult as learning a new language and culture. All they were asked to do was to kneel, along with the multitudes, before the king's image. No one would have thought any less of the young men if they simply got with the program. But they didn't kneel. They stood . . . out . . . like sore thumbs—like heretics destined for the fire.

They said to the king, "The God we serve is able to . . . rescue us. . . . But even if he does not, we want you to know, O king, that we will not serve your gods or worship the image of gold you have set up" (Daniel 3:17, 18). The young men knew there was no guarantee.

God didn't rescue Dietrich Bonhoeffer when he stood up to Hitler. God didn't rescue Dr. Martin Luther King, Jr., when he stood on a balcony in Memphis. And God didn't rescue his Son when he hung on a cross on Mount Calvary. "Even if he does not," the young men said to the king, "we won't kneel."

Everybody loves a holy war. It's easy to arm yourself against whatever the crowd has branded as evil. But it's never easy to do what's right when you are the one being branded as evil. God did rescue the young men from a fiery death. But the greatest miracle was their willingness to die. So whenever the crowd speaks, listen for the voices of peaceful dissent. Look for signs of smoke. And take note of the remains of the fire.

55

—*Dan Stuecher*

Read the story of Shadrach, Meshach, and Abednego in Daniel 3. How do you think you would have reacted if you were put in the same situation?

_____

_____

_____

_____

_____

_____

_____

_____

_____

_____

_____

_____

What are the issues in your life you know you should take a stand against, in spite of what the crowd thinks? How will you plan to be courageous for truth?

_____

_____

_____

_____

_____

_____

_____

_____

_____

_____

_____

_____

_____

Prayer

O LORD, hear my prayer,

      listen to my cry for mercy;

in your faithfulness and righteousness

      come to my relief. . . .

My spirit grows faint within me;

      my heart within me is dismayed.

I remember the days of long ago;

      I meditate on all your works

      and consider what your hands have done.

I spread out my hands to you;

      my soul thirsts for you like a parched land.

PSALM 143:1, 4–6

PRAYER

There is an organization called the "Freedom From Religion
Foundation" based in Madison, Wisconsin. I hope you've never
heard of it. Just a few years ago they mounted an effort to stop
public officials from participating in prayer breakfasts, including the annual National Prayer Breakfast in Washington, D.C.,
an event the president of the United States attends along with
thousands of political and religious leaders. A Denver judge
denied the foundation's request for a restraining order that
would forbid officials from taking part in such gatherings.
Judge Larry Naves said religion's role in American life is widely
acknowledged, and he noted that the National Prayer Breakfast
has been sponsored by congressional groups for almost 50 years.

But frankly, it doesn't require some radical fringe group to sup-
press the practice of prayer. Even without anyone trying to stop
me, there are times when I find prayer rather difficult. I hear
others pray in familiar, almost intimate speech as though they
carry God around in their hip pocket, and I wonder, "What's the
matter with me?" Oh, I can pray audibly at a moment's notice
without a problem. I can mouth the words, address them to the
Father through the name of Jesus, and sign off with an impressive
"amen." But I wonder, should we call that prayer at all?

There are times when I feel like Job in the Old Testament, trying
to find God. "If I go to the east," Job cried, "he is not there; if I
go to the west, I do not find him. When he is at work in the north,
I do not see him; when he turns to the south, I catch no glimpse
of him" (Job 23:9).

In the classic poem "The Rime of the Ancient Mariner" Samuel
Coleridge speaks for me:

> *I looked to heaven, and tried to pray;*
> *But or ever a prayer had gusht,*
> *A wicked whisper came, and made*
> *My heart as dry as dust.*

Coleridge prompts me to explore where the "wicked whisper"
comes from, and what I find isn't pretty. Sin, pride, a lack of
submission, my own pressing agendas and a hundred other
reasons all conspire against my entering God's presence through
prayer. I can only conclude that the difficulty of reaching the
goal of clear, unfettered prayer has more to do with my failures
than it does with God's distance.

61

Several years ago when Michael Ramsey was archbishop of
Canterbury, he visited the United States and was asked several
tongue-in-cheek questions only an American reporter would
dare ask:

"Have you said your prayers this morning?"
"Yes."
"What did you say in your prayers?"
"I talked to God."
"How long did you talk to God?"
"I talked to God for one minute, but it took me 29 minutes to
get there."

I often find myself among the ranks of those who take 29 minutes
to cut through all of their personal nonsense to get there. But I
have also discovered that "getting there" puts me in the only place
where life makes any sense.

—*Dan Stuecher*

Use these journal pages to write out a prayer. Putting your prayers in writing can be a helpful way to more closely connect with God.

63

A Grassy Field

If you do away with the yoke of oppression . . .

   and if you spend yourselves in behalf of the hungry

   and satisfy the needs of the oppressed,

then your light will rise in the darkness,

   and your night will become like the noonday.

ISAIAH 58:9, 10

A GRASSY FIELD

Did you know that the place where each chapter of the Bible begins and ends was decided by one person, an Englishman named Stephen Langton? He was a popular theologian who knew the Scriptures better than most during his day. In the days before the printing press, chapter divisions made it easier for those who copied the Bible by hand. Whether we agree or not with his chapter breaks, Langton made it easy for us to look up a passage like John 3:16. Stephen Langton also made our lives easier in a much greater way. In fact we owe our very freedom to this wise English preacher.

In the year 1207, the pope appointed Stephen Langton as the archbishop of Canterbury, the highest church position in England. These were the days when the pope was in a power struggle with the king. Citizens were caught in the middle. But Stephen Langton refused to be a pawn of either dictator, and he managed to use his position to rally the leading citizens of England around a summary of human rights completed in 1215. It was called the "great charter" or the Magna Carta. In a grassy field called Runnymede, near the river Thames, the king was forced to bow in acknowledgment of those rights, which are the very foundation of all democratic freedom.

The right to property, the right to representation, the right to a trial by jury—these were just some of the freedoms the U.S. Constitution inherited from theologian Stephen Langton and his Magna Carta. Granted, the Christian church has a rocky and sometimes dark history, but some of the greatest accomplishments of Western civilization have their roots clearly in the church. The road to Philadelphia passes through the place called Runnymede, a grassy field over which the shadow of Mount Calvary is firmly cast.

—*Eric Snyder for Rick Rusaw*

What are the rights and freedoms you hold most dear? How might your life be different if you were denied those rights?

What rights and freedoms do you have because you are a child of God?

_____

_____

_____

_____

_____

_____

_____

_____

_____

_____

_____

_____

Are there people in your life who are oppressed and in bondage because they don't know God's freedom? List a few names and write a short prayer for each one.

_____

_____

_____

_____

_____

_____

_____

_____

_____

_____

_____

_____

_____

Good Neighbors

Jesus replied, "'Love the Lord your God with all your heart and with all your soul and with all your mind.' This is the first and greatest commandment. And the second is like it: 'Love your neighbor as yourself.'"

MATTHEW 22:37, 38

GOOD NEIGHBORS

Robert Frost, the dean of American poets, wrote these interesting words: "Good fences make good neighbors." What do you think he meant by that? I hear a bit of a defensive ring in this statement. In other words, build good fences, establish the boundaries, don't cross those boundaries and we'll get along just fine. Keep your grass trimmed, and I'll keep my hedges cut. I'll say "Good morning" to you and you can say "How are you?" back. If you send over cookies for the kids' birthdays, I'll send over a fruitcake for Christmas. We'll be "good neighbors." But is that really what a good neighbor looks like?

A long time ago a high-powered attorney asked Jesus what makes a good neighbor. The explanation Jesus gave was considerably different from Robert Frost's. Like he did so often, Jesus told a simple story (see Luke 10) as an answer to the question.

72

A man had been ambushed by thieves as he traveled a particular road. They took everything he had, beat him, and left him for dead. Shortly, a priest happened to come by and see the man, no doubt a rather arresting sight after having been beaten to a pulp. Not about to be tarnished by the nasty circumstances or the bloody mess, the priest crossed over to the other side of the road and walked on by. Not long after that, another religious leader came by and, remarkably, the same thing happened. He saw the beaten man in the road, suffering badly and destitute. What did he do? He walked on by.

And then a Samaritan, a man from a race of people despised in those days, saw the poor man in the road, stopped, knelt down, and helped him. He bandaged him, gave him some wine, picked him up, and took him to a little inn up the road. He then entrusted the owner of the inn, a complete stranger, with enough money to take care of the man until he was healthy. If there were additional expenses, he would be back to settle up. I'm assuming you'll find it rather easy to decide which one of the three was a good neighbor.

Leave it to Jesus to select a "bottom-feeder" for the main character of his story. We know this man only as a Samaritan. But that takes us somewhere very important toward the correct meaning of neighbor. Because of his nationality we know this Samaritan was resented and held in contempt by just about everybody. He would be the very last person you and I would choose to illustrate anything!

Through the brilliance of his storytelling, Jesus had an inquiring attorney right where he wanted him. "So who was a neighbor to the man who fell into the hands of robbers?" Jesus asked. There was only one answer. "The one who had mercy on him," said the attorney. Oh, and there was one other thing Jesus said to the attorney. "Since you get it, now go do it."

—Dan Stuecher

Think about your neighbors (not just those who live near you, but also your coworkers, family, and fellow church members). What needs are apparent in their lives? Have you been stopping to help your neighbors who are hurting or in need or have you been walking right by?

Make a list of several ways you will reach out to help your neighbors this week.

_____

_____

_____

_____

_____

_____

75

_____

_____

_____

_____

_____

_____

_____

Daniel's Den of Hope

The LORD rewards every man for his righteousness and faithfulness.

DANIEL'S DEN OF HOPE

Most of us heard the story of Cassie Bernall from Columbine High School in Colorado. Two deranged students went to school one day and opened fire on their fellow students, injuring and killing innocent classmates. As he stood over Cassie with a gun pointed to her head, one gunman asked if she believed in Jesus. Cassie believed in Jesus, confessed that belief to her classmate, and was killed.

So where is the reward for faithfulness? Where is the hope in standing tall and proud for your belief in a loving God? Well, that depends on your definition of reward and hope. God's reward is a relationship with him. Cassie had it before school that morning, and she has it now. The only difference is her location. Cassie Bernall kept her commitment to God and was rewarded with Heaven.

There is another person who was asked to compromise his commitments. Daniel was a man who loved God and prayed three times a day giving thanks to him. Daniel's boss was the king of the land, Darius. Darius thought Daniel was a great employee. There was no corruption in him. He was solid. But the other employees of King Darius were jealous of Daniel, so they tricked Darius into issuing a decree that no one should pray to any god except Darius, or else be thrown into the lions' den. When Daniel learned the decree had been published, he went home to his upstairs room where the windows opened toward Jerusalem and prayed, just as he had done before.

Well, you guessed it. Darius's men found Daniel praying and told the king that his decree had been disobeyed. Darius didn't want to punish Daniel, but he had no choice. Even he wasn't above the law, and he had Daniel put into the lions' den. Again I ask, where is the reward for faithfulness?

But the next morning, when Darius and his men came to the den they found Daniel alive and well. The angel of God had shut the mouths of the lions. Darius was thrilled. He had Daniel's accusers thrown into the den, and issued a new decree that in every part of the kingdom people must fear and revere the God of Daniel. Finally, commitment was rewarded.

We tend to expect our rewards on this side of Heaven. And we don't want to wait for them. We want them now. But God doesn't view time as we do. He rewarded Daniel by shutting the mouths of lions right there on the spot, and Daniel lived. But he rewarded Cassie Bernall by taking her home to eternity, where suffering and pain no longer abide. But whether it's here on Earth, or in Heaven, this much I do know—God will reward faithfulness.

—Greg Allen

When you think about those who have been martyred for their faithfulness to God, how do you feel? How do you think those deaths make God feel?

_____

_____

_____

_____

_____

_____

_____

_____

_____

_____

_____

_____

_____

Many believers around the world today are being persecuted or martyred for their love of Christ. How do you think you would react if your life were threatened because of your faith?

_____

_____

_____

_____

_____

_____

_____

_____

_____

_____

_____

_____

_____

purpose

Alma

The righteous will flourish like a palm tree,

they will grow like a cedar of Lebanon;

planted in the house of the LORD,

they will flourish in the courts of our God.

They will still bear fruit in old age,

they will stay fresh and green,

proclaiming, "The LORD is upright;

he is my Rock."

PSALM 92:12–15

ALMA

With the overconfidence born of a fresh college diploma, I was
truly as green as green could be. On a bright summer day I
began my life of ministry with a visit to a shut-in, 85-year-old
Alma. I assumed I'd find an elderly and lonely lady living in a
dark and dingy apartment decorated with pictures of yesteryear.
Boy, was I wrong.

I knocked, Alma opened the door, and there stood a tiny bundle
of energy and joy. "Thanks for coming, Greg! Come in, come
in," she said. As Alma led me to her dining room table to talk,
I recognized the smell filling the room—homemade chocolate
chip cookies. They were delicious. My preconceived notion of
sitting in a dark apartment creating boring conversation with
a little elderly lady was so wrong. Alma's laughter, jokes, and
stories brought sunshine to the place. My college degree paled
in comparison to the diploma of experience and wisdom earned
by Alma.

As I walked out the door to go to my office (and mail back my
diploma!), Alma said, "Oh, Greg, wait a minute, I almost forgot."
She handed me another dozen of those wonderful cookies
wrapped in green plastic wrap. "Thank you so much for spending time with me today," she said. What an education. I learned
that *shut-in* didn't mean what I thought. Eighty-five-year-old
Alma taught me that, even if a person can't drive or even walk
very far, it doesn't mean that person doesn't have a life.

As a result of those summer days spent chatting with Alma, I learned the value of simply listening. We didn't have a think-tank meeting or an in-depth prayer session. We just chatted—about her husband, now gone to be with the Lord, or about my future wife. She often repeated her favorite stories. When I returned to the office, if someone asked me if I'd visited a shut-in I took offense. With a mouthful of chocolate chip cookies, I'd answer, "If you mean, was I with Alma, that wise saint, then, yes, that's where I was."

When I'm unable to drive or get out of the house and somebody calls me a shut-in, I pray that I'll have half the wisdom of Alma. I hope I'll greet the young person who visits me with warm chocolate chip cookies and old stories of joy and hope and love. I'll tell them what Jesus taught. He said we are to love God and to love people. And I'll tell them about Alma, who loved me. And when the gentle soul who visits me turns 85, I hope he'll tell the same stories to yet another young visitor, as the chain of love that is the gospel of Christ continues unbroken.

—*Greg Allen*

Have you ever visited a shut-in or a hospital patient, expecting a sad, depressed person, and instead found her full of joy? How did that experience affect you? How did you feel when you left?

_____

_____

_____

_____

_____

_____

_____

_____

_____

_____

_____

_____

_____

_____

What do you think brings such joy to people in not-so-joyful circumstances? What are some ways you can serve and encourage them (and in turn learn about the joy in their lives)?

A Double Portion

Do you not know that in a race all the runners run, but only one gets the prize? Run in such a way as to get the prize. Everyone who competes in the games goes into strict training. They do it to get a crown that will not last; but we do it to get a crown that will last forever.

1 corinthians 9:24, 25

A DOUBLE PORTION

The Bible describes extraordinary occurrences in the life of Elijah. I guess you might call him the patron prophet of long-distance runners. One time he outran the chariots of King Ahab, covering 40 miles in the process.

Willie ran like that. He was captain of his cross-country team and graduated second in his class at the naval academy. He once said, "I always had an inclination for flying," and whether it was running or taking on the challenges of a navy fighter pilot, Willie was always in front. In 1985, as a flight student at the naval air station in Pensacola, Florida, Willie ran in a 10-kilometer race that included the legendary Olympic marathon champion, Frank Shorter. Everyone expected Shorter to be the first to break the tape on that rainy March day. But Willie, like Elijah, had a different outcome in mind.

We don't know by how much Elijah outran the chariots of Ahab, but in 1985 Willie the fighter pilot outran Frank Shorter by 28 seconds. The young flight student was almost embarrassed by his victory. He told the papers he believed Shorter wasn't really trying. Shorter denied it and never forgot the modest navy pilot.

It wasn't the first time Willie had outrun a famous person. In 1979, as a teenager in Brownfield, Texas, he left a crowd of runners in the dust, including future president, George W. Bush. Like Frank Shorter, the president never forgot that young man.

And now, neither will America. The long distance runner named Willie was Commander William McCool, one of the NASA astronauts aboard the space shuttle *Columbia* on February 1, 2003.

At the end of Elijah's life, he told his protégé that when he saw Elijah depart the earth, he would inherit a double portion of his spirit. The young prophet's life would be profoundly affected by his great mentor. The protégé then watched in total shock as Elijah was carried to Heaven in a chariot of fire.

Sadly, of all the travelers in the U.S. space program, we're most aware of the ones we've lost. On February 1, 2003,we stood in shock as a chariot of fire suddenly took the seven astronauts aboard *Columbia* from us. And now, with great respect, we remember those seven souls, including Commander William McCool, the man who ran faster than Olympic great Frank Shorter and future president George W. Bush. Willie McCool, reminded all those he encountered never to hold back, but to keep on running, no matter what. And if we follow his example, we, like the protégé of Elijah, will receive a double portion of the spirit of a very good man.

91

—*Eric Snyder for Paul S. Williams*

Who has inspired you to "keep running the race" during your life's journey? What are specific things they did to encourage you?

_____

_____

_____

_____

_____

_____

_____

_____

_____

_____

_____

_____

Whom can you inspire? What specific things can you do for others to encourage them in their race?

_____

_____

_____

_____

_____

93

_____

_____

_____

_____

_____

_____

_____

Holy Leisure

*By the seventh day God had finished the work he had been doing;
so on the seventh day he rested from all his work. And God blessed
the seventh day and made it holy, because on it he rested from all
the work of creating that he had done.*

GENESIS 2:2, 3

HOLY LEISURE

"I went to the woods because I wished to live deliberately, to front only the essential facts of life, and see if I could not learn what it had to teach, and not, when I came to die, discover that I had not lived."

That was Henry David Thoreau's explanation for why, in 1845, he began living alone by a pond called Walden in Massachusetts. It just as easily could be an explanation for why many, including those in monasteries, abandon a life "frittered away by detail" and come to a place of solitude.

Those who live in monasteries are busy. They work in the world every day, managing the vineyard, serving in the community, carrying out the same tasks you and I complete on any ordinary day. But they add an element sorely lacking in most of our lives. Every morning, afternoon, evening, and night, the men who live in monasteries sing the psalms, rest in solitude, and pray.

Most of us, whether consciously or not, are engaged in the occupation of accumulation. Our goal is to build a protection against our fears and insecurities. We work 60- or 70-hour weeks to accumulate power and wealth—more power and wealth than any nation has ever known. But in the process, we distance ourselves from our hearts' desires.

For years, at least we had Sunday. Some called it the Sabbath day, borrowing a term from the Jewish calendar. Sunday was a day of rest—it was good for the soul. Stores closed. People stayed home and visited with family. At least we had one day out of every seven.

But now we work seven days a week. With the few leisure moments we do have, we escape into the trivial—mindless television shows, power toys, spectator sports—anything to deaden our senses. But it doesn't work. In the middle of the night, when you can't sleep and you're staring at the ceiling, you remember the words: "The mass of men lead lives of quiet desperation." And you are one of those desperate people.

In the midst of the mayhem of modern-day living, Thoreau suggested a way to get off the treadmill. He called it "true leisure." When we hear the word *leisure* today we think of rest and relaxation. But the meaning the church fathers gave the word long before the time of Thoreau is different. They called time off from work *otium sanctum* or "holy leisure." The aim of rest and relaxation was to put one in touch with the things that matter—family and love, nature and God. Leisure time was a chance to put one's life in perspective. When we don't take time to meditate on all that is good in our lives, we miss the holy; we miss the still small voice of God.

97

Jesus said, "What good is it for a man to gain the whole world, yet forfeit his soul?" (Mark 8:36). Were there ever words more appropriate for the American way? You may not live the life of prayer and Scripture and singing the monks enjoy or have time to retreat to Walden's Pond. But you can, with just a few prayerful moments each day, enjoy holy leisure and renew your soul.

—*Eric Snyder for Paul S. Williams*

What fills your days? Write out a typical day's schedule below.

_____

_____

_____

_____

_____

_____

_____

_____

_____

_____

_____

_____

_____

_____

Does your schedule include time for "holy leisure"? Why or why not? What specific things could you do to make time for resting in the presence of God?

99

To Play with Sweetness

"I know the plans I have for you," declares the LORD, "plans to prosper you and not to harm you, plans to give you hope and a future."

jeremiah 29:11

TO PLAY WITH SWEETNESS

She was determined to be a figure skater and a concert pianist—high ambitions for a young black girl from Birmingham, Alabama, in the 1960s. In a way, her destiny was set for her when her parents named her after an Italian musical term that means to play "with sweetness." "Sweetness" might have been her name, but do not make the mistake of assuming that she was fragile. She became quite used to adversity. As a young lady she was not allowed to use the dressing room of a department store—that was reserved for whites only. Her family attempted to eat at a restaurant after the Civil Rights Act was passed in 1964. They were greeted with silence and stares. But Sweetness did not become bitter. Instead she resolved to make a difference in the world. And make a difference she did.

The girl named Sweetness had great parents, but she credits her faith as the greatest source of her strength. The apostle Paul wrote that God "works out everything in conformity with the purpose of his will, in order that we, who were the first to hope in Christ, might be for the praise of his glory" (Ephesians 1:11, 12). Because of this hope, the bright young lady from Alabama approached each setback, each insult, and each failure as part of the wonderful script that God was writing with her. Each day she would start looking again for new opportunities. Sadly, figure skating never worked out. Becoming a concert pianist didn't pan out either. But that's because God had something else in mind for her. It's fortunate for all of us that he did.

On September 11, 2001, a voice on the telephone informed the president that the United States was under attack. It was the voice of the woman some consider the most powerful woman in America. This woman then immediately implemented emergency procedures to protect the president and his staff. She also assured the leaders of the world that the United States government was still up and running. It was the voice of the young lady from Alabama whose name in Italian means to play "with sweetness," or Condoleezza. Yes, that woman was Condoleezza Rice, our nation's National Security Advisor.

The disappointments, persecutions, and disadvantages in her life ultimately helped Condoleezza Rice find her way. The apostle Paul wrote that we "rejoice in our sufferings, because we know that suffering produces perseverance; perseverance, character; and character hope" (Romans 5:3, 4). Maybe life isn't turning out the way you wanted. But Condoleezza Rice would probably join the apostle Paul and plenty of others in saying, "Don't worry. You're in training for something better."

—Eric Snyder for Rick Rusaw

What disappointments, persecutions, and disadvantages have you faced (or are you facing right now)?

_____

_____

_____

_____

_____

_____

_____

_____

_____

_____

_____

_____

Look again at the struggles you just listed. How might each trial be preparing you for something great in the future?

_____

_____

_____

_____

_____

_____

_____

_____

_____

_____

_____

_____

_____

_____

It Starts with One Heart

Search me, O God, and know my heart;

test me and know my anxious thoughts.

See if there is any offensive way in me,

and lead me in the way everlasting.

PSalm 139:23, 24

IT STARTS WITH ONE HEART

I tend to write with a heart turned toward the good, the uplifting, and the graceful. So I don't want to shock you, but I do believe there is much wrong with this world.

Millions live in constant hunger. War, terrorism, insurrections, and hopelessness know no political boundaries. In America children aren't safe from stray bullets in their own bedrooms, and adults fear violence in their offices. Buildings tumble down and lives are snuffed out in an awful second. There is, in fact, much evil in this world.

But sometimes we become so focused on the collective ills of our society, we can be left with the impression that what goes on in one individual heart isn't all that important. As long as we fight to make a difference in the big social issues, then everything will be all right. As long as we deal with the important public issues, what difference does it make what we do in our private lives? I suppose it's a good question.

I believe the personal moral decisions I make matter a great deal. Ultimately, public morality is always a reflection of private morality. Mahatma Gandhi changed a whole culture, not because he kept his political agenda focused on the big public issues, but because he lived a personal life of self-discipline and purity. Mother Teresa's funeral brought the whole world together, not because she built a political coalition of social action, but because she served individual people on the streets of Calcutta. A carpenter from a small Middle Eastern town sacrificed his life on a Roman cross to cleanse individual hearts from sin. Gandhi, Mother Teresa, and Jesus of Nazareth all changed the world because they understood that global change begins with a single human heart.

If I want my life to make a difference, and I don't start with my own heart, I may as well not start at all. The global mirrors the personal. Private morality creates public morality. It always has and it always will.

I lived in a few midwestern suburbs before I moved to Grayson, Kentucky (population 1,600 at the time), in the 15th year of my life. It was in that small eastern Kentucky town that I learned how to change the world. I watched grown women and men live lives of simple integrity.

The week I turned 21 I listened with rapt attention to the bank president's speech about financial responsibility when he handed me my first credit card. I listened because I had watched that bank president, day in and day out, for the better part of five years, and I knew he lived with integrity.

It was in Grayson, Kentucky, that I believed my high school anatomy teacher when she told me I would go far in life. I believed her because I never heard her lie about anything or exaggerate one single truth—at school, in a Main Street store, or in church. It was in Grayson, Kentucky, that I watched my aunt and uncle work late into the night after long hard days, volunteering their time to help African missionaries. It was in Grayson, Kentucky, that I learned global change always starts in the hearts of men and women who dare to live lives of personal integrity in community with others who do the same.

I've lived in the suburbs. I've lived in a small town. I prefer small towns. Ultimately, it doesn't really matter where I live. It doesn't matter what party I belong to or what nonprofits I support. It doesn't matter how many political marches I've been a part of or how well known I am. All that matters is my heart. Because this much I know is true—real change always begins in the depths of one single human heart.

—*Paul S. Williams*

List some people in your life who have shown you what it means
to live with personal integrity. What specifically did they do that
showed those around them their pure hearts?

_____

_____

_____

_____

_____

_____

_____

_____

_____

_____

_____

_____

Who might be looking at you for an example of integrity? What might you, as one heart, do to help change the world? Write down some ideas and lift them to God in prayer.

Someone Pays a Price

Ever since I heard about your faith in the Lord Jesus and your love

for all the saints, I have not stopped giving thanks for you,

remembering you in my prayers.

EPHESIANS 1:15, 16

SOMEONE PAYS A PRICE

When I was in my twenties, more than one set of relieved parents called or wrote to thank me for being there for their wayward child. I was working with a Christian youth organization called Christ In Youth at the time, and I thought I was just doing my job. I had no idea how deeply those parents felt their words of thanks.

My own children are now in their twenties. All three are doing quite well. But the teen years were not always fun. We'll leave it at that.

For a very long time, I thought if you did a good job as a parent, you had nothing to worry about when it came to the choices your children made. I was quick to judge those parents whose children sowed wild oats by the bushel. I was wrong. The children of very good parents do not always make very good decisions.

I now have a far greater appreciation for those who are at the right place at the right time, gently guiding, cajoling, nurturing, and restoring young people who have lost their way—an old friend, a college professor, a children's church director, a young couple in their first full-time ministry. Those were some of the folks who were there for my children, providing the same encouragement my wife Cathryn and I provided to another generation 25 years ago. And I am profoundly grateful for the love they showed to Jonathan, Jael, and Jana.

None of us can survive on the faith of our parents. There comes a time when we have to face the unanswerable questions ourselves, and draw conclusions that will chart the course of our own lives. As we travel those turbulent waters, nothing is more important than our fellow travelers on the journey. Not those who *have* to be there, like Mom and Dad, but those who *choose* to be there—who choose to love because they see something in us worth loving.

John Shea, in his book *An Experience Named Spirit* tells of an old nun with red tennis shoes who brought peace into the life of an incorrigible young man. No matter how hard he pushed her away, the old nun kept coming back, until finally the young man's tough exterior façade broke, and he allowed grace and mercy into his life for the first time. It seems the old nun with the red shoes had a knack for helping wayward boys. Years of such work took their toll—loving others is hard work. Shea says, "People do change, but someone always pays the price."

To the old nun with red tennis shoes, to the psychology professor at the Christian college, to the children's church director, to my old friend, and to the young couple in the new church, to all those who have paid the price so the faith of another may grow and flourish, I say a heartfelt "Thank you."

—*Paul S. Williams*

List a few specific people who paid the price to help you change and grow in your faith. Plan to thank them personally and specifically, if possible.

List a few specific young people you know who need someone to
pay the price for them. Write a prayer for each of them, asking
God to send people into their lives—to send you, if that is his will.

_____

_____

_____

_____

_____

_____

_____

_____

_____

_____

_____

_____

_____

Dad's Retirement

Well done, good and faithful servant! You have been faithful with a few things; I will put you in charge of many things. Come and share your master's happiness!

MATTHEW 25:21

DAD'S RETIREMENT

When I told my dad I wanted to be a minister he nearly had a heart attack. Why would I want to do that? How would I support myself? Dad had other plans for me. My decision to go into ministry did not go down easily. "I'm not supporting you for the rest of your life," he said.

My father was employed by the same corporation his entire working life. He started at 19 on an assembly line and worked his way up to management. No one else in his family had ever held a job for more than a year or two. He broke old patterns, and he wanted me to go even further—to get a business degree and surpass his accomplishments. Ministry was definitely not one of the vocations on his list.

My dad ended up spending 31 years at the same company. That kind of loyalty doesn't happen much anymore. Companies no longer reward such commitment.

On the day of Dad's retirement, I arranged to fly home. Mom picked me up and we drove to Dad's office and waited at the security gate—the same security gate he had passed through day after day for more than three decades.

I stood at the security gate waiting—waiting to say thanks. Thanks for providing for your family, thanks for giving me a leg up, thanks for breaking an old family pattern, thanks for years of loyalty to your company. I stood at the security gate waiting for him to come out, just to say "Thanks."

I watched my dad walk out of his office building on his last day of work, after all those years of committed service. He walked slowly down the stairs carrying the personal items from his desk. I could only imagine the mixed emotions he felt—relief that the day was here, sadness in leaving a place and people he liked, and excitement for what was ahead. As he approached the security gate I started to applaud. He looked up to see who was causing the commotion. When he saw it was me, well, it was just one of those moments.

I took him to dinner that night, my treat. The next day we went to play golf. I paid for both of us. When he dropped me at the airport that night I told him I had covered the first two days of his retirement, but he was responsible for the rest.

A few weeks later I received a thank-you card from my dad. He had written to thank me for coming. He closed with this: "Someday life will be over for me, and I hope God will let me stand at the gate and applaud you on your last day of work. I am proud of the work you are doing."

As long as we remain faithful, someday our Father in Heaven will stand at the gate and applaud us on our last day of work, as he says "Well done."

—*Rick Rusaw*

How do you feel when you think about your retirement from working?

How do you feel when think about retiring to Heaven and hearing
God's "Well done, good and faithful servant"?

_____

_____

_____

_____

_____

_____

123

_____

_____

_____

_____

_____

_____

_____

_____

Teddy Roosevelt and Criticism

Sometimes you were publicly exposed to insult and persecution;
at other times you stood side by side with those who were so
treated. . . . So do not throw away your confidence; it will be
richly rewarded. You need to persevere so that when you have
done the will of God, you will receive what he has promised.

HEBREWS 10:33, 35, 36

TEDDY ROOSEVELT AND CRITICISM

Theodore Roosevelt was the 26th president of the United States. He was a man's man, an entrepreneur, a fearless leader, and a devoted family man. T.R., as he was often known, battled sickness as a child but eventually grew into an incredibly robust, inexhaustible powerhouse of an individual. I'm confident that he, as a forceful personality and strong leader, took enormous amounts of criticism. I've had people criticize me, and I'm sure you have too. It isn't a pleasant experience. Roosevelt had some remarkable thoughts he presented in a speech quite a few years ago. I'd like to share some of that speech with you.

He rose to speak in Paris, France, in April of 1910. The following words are characteristic of Theodore Roosevelt. He said, "It is not the critic who counts, not the man who points out how the strong man stumbled, or where the doer of deeds could have done them better. The credit belongs to the man who is actually in the arena; whose face is marred by dust and sweat and blood; who strives vigilantly; who errs and comes short again and again; who knows the great enthusiasms, the great devotions and spends himself in a worthy cause; who, at the best, knows in the end the triumph of high achievement; and who, at the worst, if he fails, at least fails while daring greatly, so that his place shall never be with those cold and timid souls who know neither victory nor defeat."

There is one thing on which most historians will agree. Teddy Roosevelt would never be criticized for being a timid soul.

It isn't a badge of honor nor is it something we should pursue to validate ourselves, but if you are living even a moderately effective life you will be criticized. Jesus said that we would have trouble in this world. There will be those who will rise up to oppose you, resist you, and complicate your life. Most often they will be removed from the actual conflict, making no sacrifice, taking no risk, but always ready to criticize you from their cheap seats above the fray.

Jesus lived an exemplary life. No, Jesus lived a perfect life. And yet, no one has ever been criticized more than he. They criticized everything about him.

If Jesus wasn't immune from criticism, how can we expect to be? Anticipate it, get used to it, and allow it to spur you on. From the example of Jesus' life and the powerful words of Teddy Roosevelt, we learn that being criticized is far better than being one of those cold, timid souls who never discovers the joy of victory after a hard-fought struggle.

—Dan Stuecher

Who are your biggest critics? What do they say?

_____

_____

_____

_____

_____

_____

_____

_____

_____

_____

_____

_____

_____

Unfair criticism can be hurtful, but constructive criticism can be helpful. Write a prayer, asking God to help you to know the difference and to react to each kind in a way that would please him.

_____

_____

_____

_____

_____

_____

_____

_____

_____

_____

_____

_____

Television Evangelist

He [Jesus] called a little child and had him stand among them.
And he said: "I tell you the truth, unless you change and become
like little children, you will never enter the kingdom of heaven.
Therefore, whoever humbles himself like this child is the greatest
in the kingdom of heaven. And whoever welcomes a little child
like this in my name welcomes me."

MATTHEW 18:2–5

TELEVISION EVANGELIST

Fred Rogers saw television for the first time in 1951 and decided to become a TV evangelist. So he went to New York to learn how TV works and then began producing a program for the nation's first public television station in Pittsburgh. During the next eight years he skipped lunch every day to attend seminary classes. He was eventually ordained with a specific charge to "broadcast grace throughout the land." His program lasted for 32 years, the longest in the history of public television. He earned four Emmys and two George Foster Peabody Awards. No one seemed to notice that it was a TV evangelist who was being honored. It takes a child to understand what Fred Rogers, "Mister Rogers," was *really* all about.

Most adults are baffled by a child's attraction to *Mister Rogers' Neighborhood.* His program is slow-paced, and he has a funny way of speaking. But children with a storm of emotional problems have been calmed by his comforting voice. There are stories of those who have suffered abuse or the lonesome burden of cerebral palsy and, through the program, found the will to live. Mothers have written about traumatized children speaking for the first time at the sight of Mr. Rogers. Countless times adults have confided that he was the only father they ever had. It's no wonder that Fred Rogers called the space between him and each viewer "holy ground." Every day he invited millions to a kingdom, a neighborhood, where, as he said, "The underlying message is that if somebody cares about you, it's possible that you'll care about others . . . and that God, in his great mercy, accepts us exactly as we are."

Fred Rogers said, "Every time I walk into the studio, I say to myself as a prayer to God, 'Let some word that is heard be yours.'" The words of his neighborhood will always be with us.

—Greg Allen

What is your first thought when you hear the words *TV evangelist?*

_____

_____

_____

_____

_____

_____

_____

_____

_____

_____

_____

_____

_____

_____

What do you think of when you think of evangelism?

_____

_____

_____

_____

_____

_____

_____

_____

_____

_____

_____

_____

_____

How does the idea that Mr. Rogers was an TV evangelist change your perspective? How could his example help you in being a witness for Jesus?

_____

_____

_____

_____

_____

_____

_____

_____

_____

_____

_____

_____

_____

_____

For the Love of a Father

Jesus . . . said, "All authority in heaven and on earth has been given to me. Therefore go and make disciples of all nations, baptizing them in the name of the Father and of the Son and of the Holy Spirit, and teaching them to obey everything I have commanded you. And surely I am with you always, to the very end of the age."

MATTHEW 28:18–20

FOR THE LOVE OF A FATHER

I have a friend who went swimming in the Hudson River, just north of New York City. It was a hot July afternoon. She was new to the area, and she docked her boat and jumped in. It didn't seem like much of a risk at the time. But later that night, as she washed the grime off her body, she noticed the polish *melting* off her fingernails. It was then she realized just how foolish she had been. What at first felt like an adventure seemed now like a really bad idea, to say the least.

I recently read about a man who went swimming in another river and risked a great deal more than taking a brief dip in the Hudson.

Nick Irons jumped into the 56-degree waters of the Mississippi River in June of 1997, to save his father's life. Nick's dad wasn't drowning. No, multiple sclerosis was crippling Nick Irons's father. Over the course of four months, Nick swam from Minneapolis to Baton Rouge, a total of 1,550 miles! He raised hundreds of thousands of dollars for MS research, and pushed the need for additional research dollars into the national news.

Nick prepared for his swim. He received vaccinations for typhoid, tetanus, and hepatitis. He recruited members of the United States Power Squadrons and Coast Guard to accompany him. But he still risked a great deal.

Nick risked boldly setting a goal and not achieving it. He risked illness and injury and pain. He risked negative press coverage, or worse yet, *no* press coverage. And he risked his career by committing several months of his life to this quest, with no guarantees of the outcome. And why did Nick Irons risk so much to swim the Mississippi? He did it because he loves his father.

There is a difference between an adventure and a quest. An adventure is something you do for the challenge of it. I've climbed a few peaks in the Rocky Mountains. I've kayaked some choppy waters off the coast of Long Island. They were fine challenges, enjoyable even. But when those adventures were done, I didn't expect to come home a changed person. I just came home with a new experience under my belt.

A quest, on the other hand, is completely different. A quest is something you're called to do, whether you want to do it or not. In J. R. R. Tolkien's great *Lord of the Rings* trilogy, Frodo Baggins was on a quest to destroy the infamous ring. The outcome was not assured. Overwhelming obstacles would lie on the path ahead. But if he succeeded, he would be changed, and many lives would be saved.

How you answer the call of a quest may well be the defining moment of your life, where your character is forged and shaped for the remainder of your days. God called his Son to a quest that no one else could take on. And Jesus took the challenge by dying on a cross for the sins of the world—and defeating death in the process. Now, Jesus calls us to our own quest—to spread his love to a dying world. Will you take the challenge?

—*Jennifer Taylor for Paul S. Williams*

Have you ever thought of God's command to tell others about Jesus as a quest, a great epic tale of heroes and dying people who need to be rescued? How does that change your perspective on sharing the gospel?

_____

_____

_____

_____

_____

_____

_____

_____

_____

_____

_____

Do you know people who need to be rescued from the bondage of sin? Write down their names and a short prayer asking for God to help you in your quest to spread his love to them.

_____

_____

_____

_____

_____

_____

_____

_____

_____

_____

_____

_____

Genius

I praise you because I am fearfully and wonderfully made;

your works are wonderful,

I know that full well.

PSALM 139:14

GENIUS

I always come away from at least one day of a business conference with my peers feeling diminished. It's my own fault. There is no one else to blame. I see the success of others, feel my own accomplishments pale in the light of their bright stars, and retreat to my hotel room to nurse my wounds. We all struggle with self-esteem, feeling others are so much more successful, more attractive, or more accomplished than we are. It's part of the human condition. But while we all struggle with self-esteem on occasion, it doesn't have to ruin our lives.

Recently I spent the better part of an afternoon with two very powerful men for whom I have the utmost respect. I learned both have a passion for motorboats—very large motorboats. Large enough that *boat* is not the operative term and *yacht* is. The two discussed Caterpillar engines, horsepower, and bow thrusters, while I thoughtfully listened.

I am an avid runner, mountain hiker, and sea kayaker. I have no piece of equipment that cost me more than $900. I'm not partial to things with motors. I like equipment that calls on *me* to be the motor. I was glad the two men were enjoying their yachting conversation. But in a rare moment of self-approval, I did not feel the need to be like them. I was perfectly happy with my touring kayak.

When I think of those I respect the most, I find they are all geniuses. And what is a genius? The word *genius* at its Latin root means simply "the spirit of a place." A genius is a person at peace with his own spirit—content to be fully and completely who he is, not who everyone else wants him to be. A genius doesn't depend on others for affirmation and approval. The author David Whyte said, "Genius is something that is itself and no other thing." Genius is at peace inside its own deeply rooted soul, whether that soul is riding in a 167-foot yacht or a 14-foot kayak.

The only way for me to become a genius is to become more fully who *I* am in God's image. If I could keep that in mind throughout every single day of my life, I'd save myself a lot of self-induced grief.

—*Paul S. Williams* 145

Who or what makes your self-esteem plummet?

_____

_____

_____

_____

_____

_____

_____

_____

_____

_____

_____

_____

_____

Does the comparison you're making with others really matter?
Is that other person really better than you in any important way?

_____

_____

_____

_____

_____

_____

_____

_____

_____

_____

_____

_____

purpose

Won't You Be My Neighbor?

Then the King will say to those on his right, "Come, you who are blessed by my Father; take your inheritance, the kingdom prepared for you since the creation of the world. For I was hungry and you gave me something to eat, I was thirsty and you gave me something to drink, I was a stranger and you invited me in, I needed clothes and you clothed me, I was sick and you looked after me, I was in prison and you came to visit me." Then the righteous will answer him, "Lord, when did we see you hungry and feed you, or thirsty and give you something to drink? When did we see you a stranger and invite you in, or needing clothes and clothe you? When did we see you sick or in prison and go to visit you?" The King will reply, "I tell you the truth, whatever you did for one of the least of these brothers of mine, you did for me."

MATTHEW 25:31, 32, 34–40

WON'T YOU BE MY NEIGHBOR?

A man had been robbed, beaten, and left half-dead by the road-side. This is how Jesus began the story of the Good Samaritan. We don't know whether the background of the thieves in the story had any role to play in their crime. Were they uneducated? Did they come from poverty? Had they no religious training? Nothing about that is mentioned. We do know, however, that two educated, prosperous, experts on the Scriptures, a priest and a Levite, saw the half-dead man on the side of the road.

For many years in Pittsburgh, Pennsylvania, there lived a man with a modern-day status equal to the priest or the Levite. His name was Dr. William Orr, an author, professor, and distinguished New Testament scholar. His knowledge of the Scriptures was unrivaled. Students came to his lectures in droves. And one day, in the dead of winter, Dr. Orr came to a man by the side of the road.

They came, they saw, and they kept walking. Both the priest and the Levite did nothing for the dying man by the roadside. "But a Samaritan, as he traveled, came where the man was; and when he saw him, he took pity on him" (Luke 10:33).

Dr. William Orr was "the most beloved professor" in the history of the institution where he served. Yet it was not his knowledge of the Scriptures or his interesting lectures that made him so loved. Education is wonderful, but it doesn't make one good. On many winter afternoons, Dr. Orr came back from his lunch freezing and without a coat. It seems that whenever he was out, he made a point of not just *seeing* the men and women by the side of the road, but caring for them, even to his own detriment. Upon his death in 1993, a facility was created in his honor and that of his wife: the William and Mildred Orr Compassionate Care Center. And though the center has helped thousands of homeless and elderly, it's only the beginning of Dr. Orr's legacy.

In answer to the question "Who is my neighbor?" Jesus indicated it was just about anybody you meet who needs help.

In his lectures Pittsburgh professor William Orr defined the word *neighbor* many times with words. But the only meaning his students remember is when he defined it with actions. The word meant a great deal to one student in particular, Fred Rogers. For over three decades, when *Mister Rogers* invited us to be his "neighbor," he was simply repeating the invitation given to him by his coatless friend and favorite professor, Dr. William Orr.

—*Greg Allen*

Would you give a needy person the coat off your back or the shoes from your feet? Why or why not?

_____

_____

_____

_____

_____

_____

_____

_____

_____

_____

_____

_____

_____

What is stopping you from being a "Good Samaritan" to your neighbors? Ask God to help you see and take the opportunities he gives you to serve others in his name.

purpose

Mind Under Matter

The L ORD *gives wisdom,*

and from his mouth come knowledge and understanding.

MIND UNDER MATTER

The king of Babylon was the most powerful man in the world. One night he had a dream. In his dream (see Daniel 4) he saw a tree that stretched as high as the sky. Its branches reached as far as the ends of the earth. In the dream an angel suddenly appeared, making a loud decree. He said, "Cut down the tree and trim off its branches; strip off its leaves and scatter its fruit. Let the tree be a stump in a grassy field, drenched with dew and living among the animals and plants." The king, whose name was Nebuchadnezzar, asked for someone to interpret his strange dream. None of his counselors were able to do so, except for his chief adviser, a Jewish prophet named Daniel. When Daniel heard the king's dream he was very troubled. He said, "If only the meaning of your dream applied to your enemies." And that's when Daniel delivered to Nebuchadnezzar the bad news.

He said, "You are the tree, O King. For you have become great and strong. But you will soon lose that which you believe to be the source of your power." The king had great military might. Daniel could have said that a greater army would invade Babylon and overthrow the kingdom. But that's not what he said was going to happen. Babylon was very prosperous. The prophet could have said a devastating flood, fire, or earthquake was coming to wipe

Babylon away. But that isn't what he said either. He told the king that what was going to happen would last until Nebuchadnezzar understood that "the Most High is sovereign over the kingdoms of men and gives them to anyone he wishes." The king would not lose his life, his army, his economy, or anything that was associated with Babylon the Great. Yet what he was about to lose was worth more to him than any of those things.

The king of Babylon had reasoned that it was his own brilliant mind that built and sustained his kingdom. Nebuchadnezzar, however, was about to discover that he had no more a grasp on power than he did on the weather. "You will no longer be rational," Daniel the prophet said to him, "but you will live and behave like an animal." A year later the king suddenly went mad, and for seven years he lived like a beast, eating grass for food. What's even more remarkable is that Babylon continued functioning without him. When his madness ended, he humbly assumed his place as king once again. Nebuchadnezzar learned from his experience that the power of his position had very little to do with himself and had everything to do with the God who put him into power.

—*Eric Snyder for Rick Rusaw*

Who are the Nebuchadnezzars of our day—leaders who see their own wisdom and intelligence as the only reason for their power and success? What would need to happen to turn these leaders to God?

_____

_____

_____

_____

_____

_____

_____

_____

_____

_____

_____

_____

From where do your success, intelligence, and wisdom come?
Do you show others by the way you live that you know those
things are from God?

_____

_____

_____

_____

_____

_____

_____

_____

_____

_____

_____

_____

_____

Heroes with Feet of Clay

> *God, who said, "Let light shine out of darkness," made his light*
> *shine in our hearts to give us the light of the knowledge of the*
> *glory of God in the face of Christ. But we have this treasure in jars*
> *of clay to show that this all-surpassing power is from God and*
> *not from us.*

2 CORINTHIANS 4:6, 7

HEROES WITH FEET OF CLAY

When I was a kid I scoured every shelf at the Akron Public Library for books about Abraham Lincoln. We had visited his birthplace in Kentucky, and that kindled the fires of my fascination with America's favorite president.

When he was a young child, Lincoln spent an entire winter with his family in a three-sided shed. I could never quite understand why his dad didn't haul himself outside on a nice winter day and build a fourth side. Whatever the case, Lincoln also did his home-work by firelight. When he worked in a store, he walked miles to give the correct change to a customer he had inadvertently shortchanged. These were the stories that stayed in a boy's heart.

But as difficult as his childhood was, Lincoln rose above it. He worked the Mississippi, moved to Indiana and Illinois, failed at love, failed at politics, and with his gangly appearance and high-pitched voice, he appeared headed for a life of unremarkable mediocrity. But Lincoln persevered and became the sixteenth president of the United States. And though the awfulness of the Civil War befell his presidency, Abraham Lincoln rose to the occasion and held a fragile nation together. He was a true hero.

All the books I had read about Lincoln as a child made him seem bigger than life. So when I visited the Lincoln Memorial in Washington, D.C., the size of the statue seemed just about right. That was the Lincoln I had come to know and admire— way bigger than life.

Of course, Abraham Lincoln was not bigger than life. When I graduated to the adult section of the library, I began to read the books that showed another side of Mr. Lincoln. Among many other problems, he struggled mightily with depression. The man who gave us the most inspiring address in American history found it hard to get out of bed in the morning.

But of course, Lincoln was not alone among heroes. All heroes have a shadow side. By most descriptions, Mahatma Gandhi was not a very good father, and he could be petty with his assistants. Thomas Jefferson seemed to have a remarkable capacity to deceive himself when it suited his political agenda. They were heroes with feet of clay. And therein lies the hope.

The older I get, the more conscious I become of the failures of my own life—my occasions of arrogance, my desperate need to be liked by everyone, my own dark moods, the ways in which I have failed my wife and children. But there is no hope in focusing on my failures. The most difficult climb is the climb out of the pit of self-loathing. Leo Tolstoy, after giving the world *War and Peace,* one of the finest novels ever written, ended his life in an ever-deepening cycle of self-loathing. He was a perfectionist who could never make himself good enough in the eyes of his own stern conscience.

163

But Gandhi, Jefferson, Lincoln, and many other heroes with feet of clay didn't descend into the pit of self-loathing. They came to look beyond their shadow sides to see the difference they could make on their better days. They found the character beneath their flaws and offered it up to make the world a better place than the one they had found. They became heroes because, above all else, they focused on the good, the beautiful, the redemptive, and the possible.

And in so doing, they showed me how to live.

—*Paul S. Williams*

Who were your heroes as a child? What flaws did you find out about them later in life? Did that change your outlook on their hero status?

What are some of your own character flaws that cause you to struggle? What are the strengths God has given you that allow you to serve him in spite of your faults?

_____

_____

_____

_____

_____

_____

_____

_____

_____

_____

_____

_____

_____

_____

Of Dogs and God

Greater love has no one than this, that he lay down his life for his friends.

OF DOGS AND GOD

I have a golden retriever at home named Lilly. Well actually, she's my daughter Jana's dog, but we won't quibble over ownership. She is the sweetest dog that ever lived. I take her on hour-long runs in the wintertime and 20-minute jogs in the summer, when it's too hot for her to run farther. She puts her head hard against my leg when I'm sitting on the couch and won't move an inch until I scratch behind her ears. When I come in the house after a trip, she cries and cries, then rolls over on the floor and waits for me to scratch her belly. And I'm not sure, but I think I just might be willing to jump in front of a bus to save that dog.

Now I know I'm going to get myself in trouble, but here goes. I have never felt the same way about my cat.

We had a beautiful Maine coon cat before our son was born. His name was Fred. He would come running into the kitchen at the sound of the can opener, and he sat on a chair in the living room and looked out the front window. He never climbed in the Christmas tree, and after our first child was born, he tolerated his pokes and jabs without retribution. But I never felt nearly as attached to that cat as I do to my dog. I never once had the sense that my cat needed me. He always seemed independent. He tolerated me, as long as the can opener kept whirring. But I had no doubt that his ideal life would be spent alone, stalking prey in the woods.

My dog, on the other hand, definitely needs me. Dogs understand community. The family hierarchy is clear and unmistakable, and every dog knows his or her place in it. And that's the point. A dog knows its life is dependent on the pack. It knows it can't live independently. It doesn't want to live independently. The dog wants to live with me and please me. It's in her nature to do so. And that's why I'd probably meet the grill of a Greyhound bus if it meant saving that mutt.

My dog knows what I sometimes forget. God created us to live in community. He wants me to be living in a community of loving people who care deeply about one another. He wants me to please others, and to be pleased when others please me. He wants me to know just how dependent I am on those around me. And he wants me to nurture and cherish those relationships. I'm not an independent entity, hiding in the brush, stalking prey. I am a created being who needs to love and be loved. And God is the same way. He too lives in community with the Son and the Spirit, and He needs to love and be loved. And yes, there's no doubt about it. He would in fact meet the grill of a Greyhound bus if it meant saving me.

—Paul S. Williams

169

What does it mean to be a part of a community? List some of your specific ideas about what a community does and looks like.

_____

_____

_____

_____

_____

_____

_____

_____

_____

_____

_____

_____

_____

Most likely you'll never be asked to actually die for a friend, but in
what ways can you love others by laying down your life for them?

_____

_____

_____

_____

_____

_____

_____

_____

_____

_____

_____

_____

_____

Love My Neighbor?

If you have any encouragement from being united with Christ, if any comfort from his love, if any fellowship with the Spirit, if any tenderness and compassion, then make my joy complete by being like-minded, having the same love, being one in spirit and purpose. Do nothing out of selfish ambition or vain conceit, but in humility consider others better than yourselves. Each of you should look not only to your own interests, but also to the interests of others.

PHILIPPIANS 2:1–4

LOVE MY NEIGHBOR?

Jesus told stories more than he gave tests. But he wasn't above giving a test or two when it was the only way to drive home a point. On three different occasions, intelligent, erudite, well-educated people asked Jesus how to get into Heaven. All three times Jesus gave the same very simple answer—love God and love your neighbor. But, of course, simple doesn't necessarily mean easy.

I used to have a neighbor who swatted flies outdoors. That's right. Outdoors. Now if a fly is in my house, I figure I have a right to swat the fly. It's my house. But when we're outside, isn't that the fly's house? Nevertheless, my neighbor swatted flies outdoors.

For years we had a neighbor who usually got inside his front door before he fell down drunk. Usually. Unfortunately, on many occasions he used to be lying in the front yard, yelling at my very young children to help him into the house—made them feel really secure about their neighborhood.

You know, there's a saying of the desert monks that really bothers me. It goes like this: "If a man settles in a certain place and does not bring forth the fruit of the place, the place itself will cast him out."

Maybe that's what Jesus had in mind when he said I should love my neighbor. But tell me honestly—how in the world am I supposed to love those neighbors? How can I bring forth the fruit of my place? What does that fruit look like?

How can I love my neighbors? Well, for me the first step was getting to know them by listening to them. The man who swatted flies took care of his wife through a long illness. After her death, he turned his attention to his two pug dogs. When the dogs were in the backyard, he wanted to keep the flies off them, so he swatted flies. It probably didn't do much good, but it kept him busy through his long, sad days.

The alcoholic next door died a very lonely death. Through the years I got to know him just a bit when I helped him into the house. He never had the strength to take us up on our offer to help him any further. I did get to help one of his drinking buddies even more. He told me a lot about my neighbor and what a fine friend he had been to him through the years, until alcohol got the best of both of them.

My neighbors were hurting people with sad stories and great needs. The same is true of your neighbors. Behind every life there is a compelling story, if only we would have ears to hear and hearts to care.

—*Paul S. Williams*

175

What people around you seem frightening or strange? List
some ideas of why they might be this way.

_____

_____

_____

_____

_____

176

_____

_____

_____

_____

_____

_____

_____

_____

How might you find out about the needs and hurts of those people?
In what ways can you help them know that God loves them?

_____

_____

_____

_____

_____

_____

_____

_____

_____

_____

_____

_____

'77

purpose

Giving Hope to Others

Encourage one another and build each other up.

1 Thessalonians 5:11

GIVING HOPE TO OTHERS

Todd recently moved from Kentucky to California. Wow, what a change: from the midwest to the west coast; from tractor pulls to surfboards; from fried catfish to sushi. Todd and his wife have just taken a major leap of faith into a different culture. He left a job where he was one of many in order to be the lone ranger leader of a new corporation. What a change.

Is Todd alone in California? No. Before he even agreed to leave the safe confines of the Bluegrass State, Todd spent time in California talking with others who made a commitment to help him get his company off the ground. They would help supply personnel, finances, and encouragement. They'd even give Todd's wife and children a place to meet other mommies and children so they could make new friends. All of a sudden the story of Kentucky to California is looking pretty good, isn't it? You know why? Hope. Todd has been assured of all the necessary support to provide his family with enough hope to make it, even in a strange new land.

Wouldn't it be wonderful to find more Todds in the world and give them the support they need? I'm not talking about daring business geniuses as much as those neighbors and friends who just need to be held up every now and again. Take Moses for example. Right, Moses, that phenomenal leader who saw the Red Sea part with the raising of his staff. His life didn't always read like a success story. As a matter of fact, Exodus 17 gives the account of Moses' army fighting an enemy, and losing. The Bible says as long as Moses held up his staff the Israelites were winning, but if the staff went down, they'd begin to lose. Just as they were crushing the enemy under Moses' raised staff, Moses got tired, lost the energy in his arms, and down came the staff and the army.

Then came a support structure that gave hope—two men named Aaron and Hur. They held up Moses' tired arms and raised the staff. The army regained momentum and defeated the enemy. The key to this story was not the skill and genius of the leader but the support provided by his friends.

So what do Todd and Moses have in common? They both had a need for hope. But where does hope come from? There are those instances where God intervenes and gives hope in person, to be sure, but it seems most common for God to provide hope through the support of a friend—a friend who lifts up tired arms in times of trouble. Maybe you need to be that friend. Maybe you need to put aside your own concerns for a while and look for a friend whose arms are falling. And when you find that friend, lift him up.

—*Greg Allen*

Name people who held you up when you struggled. What specific things did they do for you? Have you ever thanked them?

_____

_____

_____

_____

_____

_____

_____

_____

_____

_____

_____

_____

_____

Who needs you to hold them up right now? List one or two people and write a prayer for each of them as a way to begin reaching out to them in their struggles.

_____

_____

_____

_____

_____

_____

_____

_____

_____

_____

_____

_____

_____

WINDOWS OF WORSHIP™

Devotions in this book are based on scripts first delivered by Paul Williams and the following hosts for *Worship*.

GREG ALLEN is a worship minister at Southeast Christian Church in Louisville, Kentucky, where he has served since 1983.

RICK RUSAW is senior minister at LifeBridge Christian Church in Longmon Colorado, where he has served since 1991.

DAN STUECHER is senior minister at Harborside Christian Church in Safety Harbor, Florida, a congregation he founded in 1984.

Be sure to read and give these other Windows of Worship™ devotional journals

ISBN 0-7847-1515-7
25002

ISBN 0-7847-1516-5
25003